INVESTIGATING NOISE POLLUTION

CYNTHIA KENNEDY HENZEL

Wonder Books
An Imprint of The Child's World®
childsworld.com

The Child's World
childsworld.com

Published by The Child's World®
800-599-READ • www.childsworld.com

Photography Credits
Photographs ©: Shutterstock Images, cover, 2, 11 (alarm clock), 11 (person), 11 (fireworks), 11 (semicircle), 13, 14, 24, 26, 29; iStockphoto, 5, 15, 17; William Perugini/Shutterstock Images, 6; Eddie Hernandez/Shutterstock Images, 8; Pisa Photography/Shutterstock Images, 9; Sergey Mastepanov/Shutterstock Images, 11 (washing machine); Green Pic Studio/Shutterstock Images, 11 (airplane); Craig R. J. D./iStockphoto, 19; Pavlo Glazkov/Shutterstock Images, 21; RT Images/Shutterstock Images, 23; Jakapong Paoprapat/Shutterstock Images, 27; Prostock Studio/Shutterstock Images, 31

ISBN Information
9781503858121 (Reinforced Library Binding)
9781503860100 (Portable Document Format)
9781503861466 (Online Multi-user eBook)
9781503862821 (Electronic Publication)

LCCN 2021952370

Printed in the United States of America

BRINGING THE WORLD TO YOUNG READERS 1968

ABOUT THE AUTHOR

Cynthia Kennedy Henzel has a bachelor's degree in social studies education and a master's degree in geography. She has written more than 100 books and 150 stories for young people.

Typically, there is more noise pollution in the city than in the countryside.

TABLE OF CONTENTS

CHAPTER ONE

MAKING IT HARD TO THINK

Nadia squirmed in her seat. The teacher was explaining what to study for the next test. Nadia tried to pay attention, leaning forward to hear better. It was 1972 and she was in sixth grade. This year seemed much harder than the last. She felt tired and had trouble paying attention. Her grades had gone down.

Outside, an **elevated** train roared by. It was really loud. The teacher stopped talking and waited for the train to pass. This was not unusual. Nadia's school was near a train track in Manhattan. Her classroom was on the side of the building next to the tracks.

Noise pollution can make students feel tired and stressed.

Sometimes, fast trains came by every couple minutes. When trains passed, the teacher had to shout to make students hear her. Usually, the teacher stopped talking until the train was gone. Then she brought the class back to attention until the next train went past.

Nadia talked to her mother about the noise problem at school. Her mother was worried. She talked to the other parents and teachers.

The continuous noise from passing trains negatively affects people's concentration. It can also cause headaches.

They pointed out the noise to the city. But no one did anything about it. Finally, some of the parents decided to take the city to court. They hired lawyers to help. The lawyers knew they needed proof that the noise harmed the students. So experts did a study.

The results showed that sixth grade students on the quiet side of the building had better grades than sixth grade students near the train tracks. This information eventually got the attention of the city.

The city agreed to make changes. Four years later, the school added **insulation** on the ceilings. This made the classrooms quieter. Soon, sixth grade students learning near the tracks were getting better grades. They were less tired and could pay better attention in class.

The world is a noisy place. People are surrounded by noise from traffic, music, people talking, sirens, and hundreds of other sounds. People do not pay attention to a lot of the sounds around them. But it does not matter whether people think about the sounds. The brain records what the ears hear.

People living in a city may experience noise pollution so often that they no longer notice it.

The U.S. Environmental Protection Agency, also called EPA, is responsible for studying noise pollution in the United States. The EPA defines noise pollution as unwanted or **disturbing** sound. Some scientists believe that noise pollution is second only to air pollution in harming people's health.

CHAPTER TWO

TOO MUCH NOISE

Millions of people live in cities. They may hear constant traffic sounds. This can include cars honking and brakes screeching. There is also noise from construction. Airplanes roar as they fly overhead. The sounds of leaf blowers or lawn mowers rumble through the air. People chatter as they cross the street, and music booms from cars.

People living in cities can have a higher risk of hearing loss.

Sounds may seem loud to some people but not to others. For example, some people like listening to loud music. But loud music may be noise pollution to their neighbors. Scientists measure how loud a sound is in units called decibels (dB). Zero dB is a sound that humans can hardly hear. A refrigerator humming is 40 dB. A normal conversation is approximately 50 to 60 dB. Sounds at these levels do not damage the ears or annoy most people.

THE AUDIOMETER

In the late 1800s, Alexander Graham Bell invented the telephone. He also invented the audiometer. This is the instrument used to test hearing. Bell was interested in sound because his mother and wife were deaf. Bell Telephone Laboratories invented the decibel scale so they could tell how loud the volume was over the telephone. They named the decibel in honor of Alexander Graham Bell.

LEVELS OF NOISE

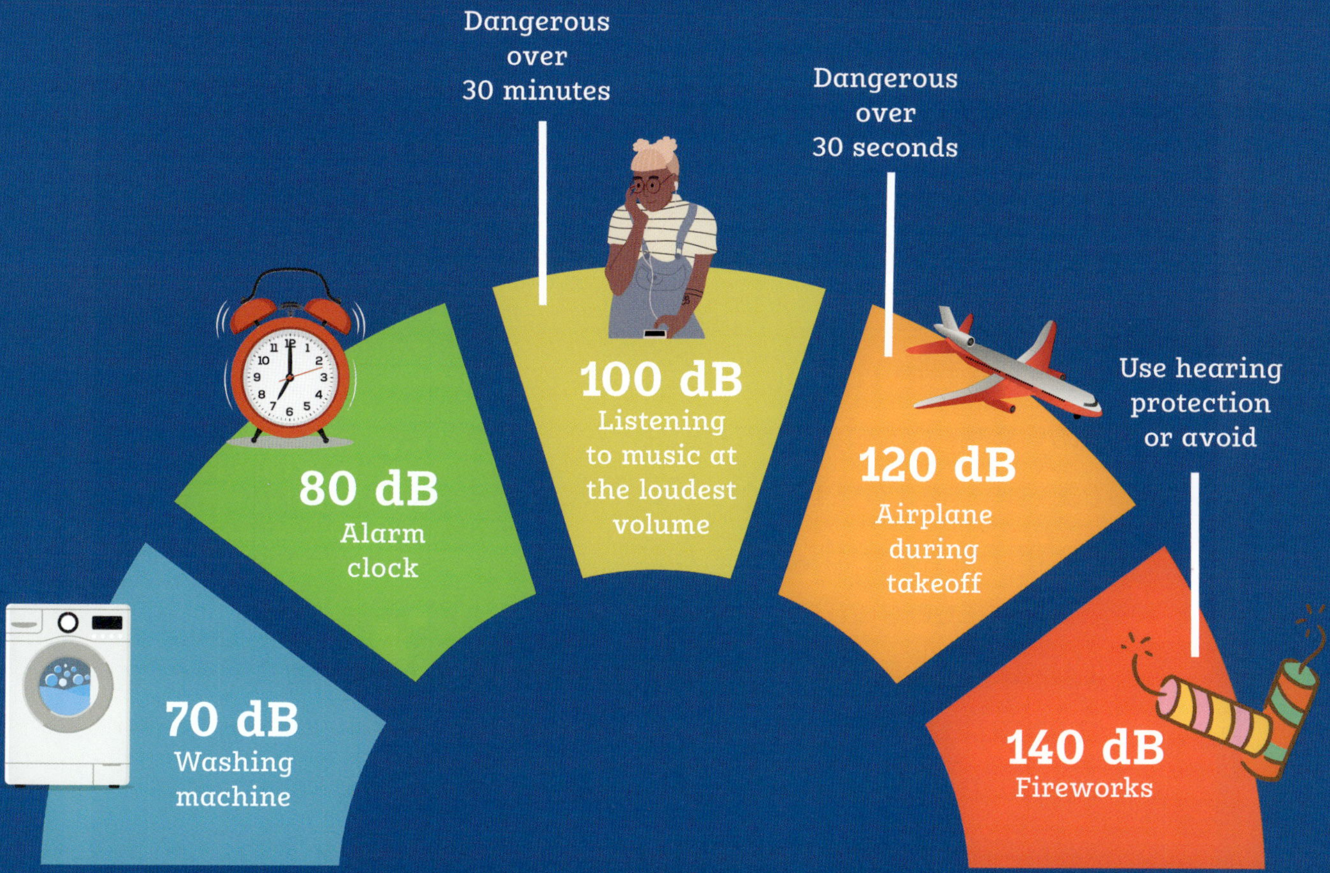

People experience different levels of noise every day. Some types of noise can be dangerous when a person is around the noise for a long enough time.

A dishwasher has a noise level of 70 dB. A car driving in a city will have a noise level of 80 to 85 dB. Many people find this level of noise annoying.

Noise levels above 85 dB are dangerous. This level of noise can damage the ears after listening to it for about two hours. These include the roar of leaf blowers and lawn mowers. Loud sporting events and nearby car horns can reach 100 dB. This can cause hearing loss after 15 minutes.

Concerts can reach a noise level of 105 to 110 dB. This can damage a person's hearing in five minutes. Noise with 120 dB or more, like standing near a firecracker, is painful and will cause immediate damage to the ears.

Scientists recommend that the noise level at home should be 35 dB at night and 40 dB during the day. Sounds louder than 55 dB may be harmful over a period of time. But many people live in areas where the noise level is more than 70 dB.

On average, construction sounds are around 90 dB.

CHAPTER THREE

NOISE KILLS

Noise pollution not only harms people's ears. It also affects people's health in other ways. Some people can sleep through noise. But sometimes noise wakes people up. Whether a person is awake or asleep, the body responds to noise. A good night's sleep is important to a person's health. People who do not get enough sleep often feel tired all day. They have trouble remembering things or doing simple tasks.

Noise pollution can affect people's sleeping patterns.

Neighborhoods can get noisy when construction happens nearby.

People may get less fresh air and exercise if it is too noisy outside. They might keep their windows closed. They do not spend time in their yards because it is too noisy. They may stay inside where it is quiet rather than take a walk. One study conducted a survey of homeowners and renters in the United States. About half of the people who participated thought their neighborhoods were too noisy. Approximately one-third of the people wanted to move to get away from the noise.

Noise pollution raises people's level of stress. This may make people feel anxious or put them in a bad mood. Stress releases a **hormone** called cortisol. Cortisol prepares the body to defend itself by running away or fighting. It does this by affecting how the blood flows throughout the body.

Noise does not only affect how people feel mentally. It affects physical health as well. People **exposed** to noise pollution over time have more diseases related to blood flow.

HEARING TOO WELL

Too much loud noise can cause deafness. Loud noises can also cause ears to become extra **sensitive** to sounds. People with hyperacusis (hy-pur-uh-KYOO-sis) have overly sensitive hearing. Even normal sounds like a dropped spoon can seem painfully loud. Hyperacusis can be caused by ear infections, experiencing a loud noise (such as a gunshot), or long-term exposure to noise. Another ear problem, tinnitus, sounds like a buzzing or ringing in the ears. Tinnitus is most often caused by exposure to loud sounds.

Adults can help protect children's ears by giving them earmuffs in loud spaces.

These include heart disease, diabetes, and high blood pressure. A 10 dB increase in noise from traffic can increase heart disease by up to 17 percent. These diseases may take years off someone's life. A study from Europe found that noise pollution caused 48,000 new cases of heart disease and 12,000 early deaths each year.

Children are more sensitive to noise pollution than adults. Hearing loss from noise at an early age can lead to speech problems. Plus, hearing loss due to noise cannot be corrected. Once the ears are damaged, the problem cannot be solved by medicine or surgery.

Noise pollution also affects children's ability to learn. Children exposed to traffic and airport noise for a long time have poorer memories and poorer grades on tests. Children exposed to noise pollution have more problems paying attention while reading.

CHAPTER FOUR

NOISE AND THE ENVIRONMENT

Noise pollution is also harmful to animals. Many animals have much more sensitive hearing than humans. Noise pollution keeps them from communicating and finding food.

It is harder for bats to find prey in cities.

Some animals use sound to hunt for prey. For example, bats make high screeching noises. The sound bounces off objects, including insects, to help the bats find food. But bats are less successful hunters in areas with too much noise pollution.

Owls have very sensitive ears. They use their ears to hunt. People can barely detect a change in volume of 1 dB. But researchers found that a 1 dB increase in noise meant owls were 8 percent less likely to find food.

Many types of birds avoid noisy places, but they will come back when the areas get quieter. People saw this happen in 2020. That year, COVID-19 spread around the world. Millions of people got sick. Most cities closed shops and schools to help stop the spread. As a result, the streets became much quieter. Traffic noise became 8 to 20 percent lower than normal. Within two weeks, many birds moved closer to the airports and highways.

Ruby-throated hummingbirds were three times more likely to be seen near airports during the pandemic.

Noise pollution even affects animals under the sea. It is hard to see very far underwater, so many sea creatures use sound to communicate with each other. They also use sound to hunt for prey. The ears of whales and dolphins are much more sensitive than human ears.

The constant flow of ships across the ocean creates a lot of underwater noise. Plus, people who are mapping the ocean floor make loud noises.

Many bustling cities all around the world became quieter during the spread of COVID-19.

The people mapping use air guns to bounce sound off of the ocean floor. This lets them find the depth of different parts of the ocean. Orca whales may travel 5,800 miles (9,300 km) each year. However, noise pollution can **interfere** with the orca's ability to travel and stay safe.

People have studied what happens when the noise stops. On September 11, 2001, the World Trade Center in New York was attacked by terrorists. Almost all worldwide shipping stopped as airports and ports closed to prevent another terror attack. Noise pollution in the sea dropped to almost nothing. Scientists found that the stress hormones in whales also dropped.

When airports close, there is a lot less noise pollution from airplane engines and crowds.

CHAPTER FIVE

QUIETING DOWN

People can protect their ears from loud noises by wearing earplugs. But it is not practical to wear earplugs all the time. The best solution for noise pollution is to reduce the cause of the noise.

The biggest cause of noise pollution in cities is transportation. There are many things that cities can do to reduce traffic noise. Cities can encourage people to use electric cars and trains. Although electric vehicles are not silent, they make a lot less noise than gas engines.

When in a loud environment, people can wear earplugs to protect their ears.

Cities can also encourage more people to walk or bike. One way to do this is to build more safe and pleasant walkways and bike lanes.

Building walls along roadways can decrease sound. Cities can spend money to insulate homes against noise pollution. In addition, new ways of using **asphalt** can reduce noise up to 6 dB. Asphalt roads can be made quieter by adding rubber to the mix. They can also be made quieter by changing the size of particles in the asphalt mix or pouring the asphalt with more air spaces.

ELECTRIC CARS AND NOISE

Electric cars can solve much of the noise pollution from traffic but not all of it. Over half of the noise from traffic comes from the sound of tires on pavement. This is especially true of traffic on freeways. The faster a car goes, the more noise the tires make. But where traffic is slower, electric cars can help reduce noise levels.

Walls built along highways help to reduce the traffic sounds people can hear from nearby houses.

Although the EPA studies the effects of noise pollution, it is the job of states and local communities to pass and enforce laws dealing with noise. Laws can limit when people are allowed to make noise. This might include turning down the music at night. Laws could stop cities from doing street repair or trash collection when people are sleeping. Cities can create quiet zones, such as parks, where noise is limited. This gives people a quiet place to spend time outside.

Everyone can help reduce noise. They can turn down their music or television. People can plant trees or build fences that block noise from busy streets. They can use rugs on the floor and thick curtains on the windows. People can also put bookcases on noisy walls. They can even help educate others about the dangers of noise pollution.

Noise is an invisible pollution. Most people do not realize the harm it causes. Paying attention to noise pollution can make people happier and healthier.

People can take a break from noisy cities and neighborhoods by going into nature.

FAST FACTS

- Noise pollution is unwanted or disturbing sound.
- Noise is measured in units called decibels (dB).
- Hearing loss can result from very loud noises or long exposure to medium noises.
- Noise pollution causes loss of sleep. It can also increase stress and the chances of getting heart disease.
- Children are more sensitive to noise than adults.
- Noise pollution causes speech and learning problems in children.
- Animals on land and in the sea are affected by noise pollution. It hurts their abilities to communicate, navigate, and find food.
- Transportation is the most significant noise polluter in cities.
- Cities can decrease noise pollution by encouraging quieter transportation such as using electric vehicles, walking, and biking.
- Cities can help reduce traffic noise with better-insulated buildings and soundproof barriers.

WHAT PEOPLE HEAR

MATERIALS

- Paper for recording sounds
- Pencil

DIRECTIONS

1. For ten minutes, three times a day, carefully observe the sounds around you.
2. After ten minutes, write down what you heard.
3. At the end of the day, compare your notes about the noises you heard. Think about whether the sounds were quiet or loud. Then think about whether they were normal or unusual. Which of these sounds contributed to noise pollution? What types of sounds bothered you? Write down your findings.

GLOSSARY

asphalt (AS-fawlt) Asphalt is a sticky, black substance used to pave roads. Roads paved with asphalt can get really hot in the summer.

disturbing (dihs-TURB-ing) Disturbing means bothering someone or causing anxiety. The loud music was disturbing as he studied.

elevated (EL-uh-vay-ted) Elevated means raised higher. The train track was elevated above the streets.

exposed (ex-POHZD) Exposed means something is not protected. Her ears were exposed to loud music.

hormone (HOR-mohn) A hormone is a chemical in the body that affects the activity of cells. Cortisol is a stress hormone.

insulation (in-suh-LAY-shun) Insulation is a material used in buildings to reduce outside noise. Good insulation in houses helps to block city noises.

interfere (in-tur-FEER) To interfere means to prevent something from happening. Too much noise may interfere with studying.

sensitive (SEN-sah-tiv) Sensitive means easily affected, sometimes in a negative way. He was sensitive to traffic noises.

WAYS YOU CAN HELP

- Walk or ride a bike instead of traveling in a car.
- Protect your ears by turning down the volume when listening to music.
- Research noise pollution in your community and talk to your class about what you find.

FIND OUT MORE

In the Library

Amstutz, L. J. *How Can We Reduce Transportation Pollution?* Minneapolis, MN: Lerner, 2016.

Honders, Christine. *Sound: It's Energetic*. New York, NY: PowerKids Press, 2020.

Slingerland, Janet. *Quiet vs. Loud*. Mankato, MN: The Child's World, 2021.

On the Web

Visit our website for links about investigating noise pollution: **childsworld.com/links**

Note to Parents, Teachers, and Librarians: We routinely verify our Web links to make sure they are safe and active sites. So encourage your readers to check them out!

INDEX